AF428040

CONTENTS

COMPUTER NETWORK APPLICATIONS USING GAME THEORY

Computer Network Applications

DR. T.P. ANITHAASHRI,

Professor & Head, Dept. of Cloud Computing,

Saveetha School of Engineering,

Saveetha Institute of Medical and Technical Sciences,

Chennai, Tamilnadu, INDIA

Copyright © Dr. T.P. Anithaashri
All Rights Reserved.

This book has been self-published with all reasonable efforts taken to make the material error-free by the author. No part of this book shall be used, reproduced in any manner whatsoever without written permission from the author, except in the case of brief quotations embodied in critical articles and reviews.

The Author of this book is solely responsible and liable for its content including but not limited to the views, representations, descriptions, statements, information, opinions and references ["Content"]. The Content of this book shall not constitute or be construed or deemed to reflect the opinion or expression of the Publisher or Editor. Neither the Publisher nor Editor endorse or approve the Content of this book or guarantee the reliability, accuracy or completeness of the Content published herein and do not make any representations or warranties of any kind, express or implied, including but not limited to the implied warranties of merchantability, fitness for a particular purpose. The Publisher and Editor shall not be liable whatsoever for any errors, omissions, whether such errors or omissions result from negligence, accident, or any other cause or claims for loss or damages of any kind, including without limitation, indirect or consequential loss or damage arising out of use, inability to use, or about the reliability, accuracy or sufficiency of the information contained in this book.

Made with ♥ on the Notion Press Platform
www.notionpress.com

ACKNOWLEDGEMENT

This book is based on my research in the field of Computer Network applications using Game Theory in College of Engineering, Anna University, Chennai. I would like to express my sincere gratitude to my Mom T.P. Eswari who was my inspiration and support to write this book. I am grateful to my beloved Director Mam Dr. Ramya Deepak, Saveetha School of Engineering, SIMATS, Chennai, who motivated me to complete this journey. Finally, I express heartful thanks to my hubby, daughters, brothers, sisters, friends and gurus without their support this would have not been possible.

PREFACE

This book deals with the usage of game theory in computer network applications. Chapter 1 explains the basic concept of game theory. Chapter 2 represents the various game strategies and its application through illustrations. Chapter 3 explains the concept of finitely and infinitely repeated games, by specifying the different game strategy with pay-offs factors. Chapter-4 specifies network applications in which how game theory is used in network applications and helps to evaluate the performance of computer network through the service offerings for various applications. Chapter 5 specifies the strategies to handle the perfect and imperfect information in network applications.

Chapter 1

INTRODUCTION

A mathematical formulation makes it easy to define concepts precisely, to verify the consistency of ideas, and to explore the implications of assumptions. Consequently our style is formal: we state definitions and results precisely, interspersing them with motivations and interpretations of the concepts. The use of mathematical models creates independent mathematical interest. In this book, however, we treat game theory not as a branch of mathematics but as a social science whose aim is to understand the behavior of interacting decision-makers; we do not elaborate on points of mathematical interest. From our point of view the mathematical results are interesting only if they are confirmed by intuition.

The models of game theory are highly abstract representations of classes of real-life situations. Their abstractness allows them to be used to study a wide range of phenomena. For example, the theory of Nash equilibrium has been used to study oligopolistic and political competition. The theory of mixed strategy equilibrium has been used to explain the distributions of tongue length in bees and tube length in flowers. The theory of repeated games has been used to illuminate social phenomena like threats and promises. The theory of the core reveals a sense in which the outcome of trading under a price system is stable in an economy that contains many agents. The boundary between pure and applied game theory is vague; some developments in the pure theory were motivated by issues that arose in applications. Nevertheless we believe that such a line can be drawn. Though we hope that this book appeals to those who are interested in applications, we stay almost entirely in the territory of "pure" theory. The art of applying an abstract model to a real-life situation should be the subject of another tome. Game theory uses mathematics to express its ideas formally. However, to generic individuals. "They" has many merits as a singular pronoun, although its use can lead to ambiguities (and complaints from editors).

1.1 Game Theory

A game is characterized by a set of rules having a certain formal structure, governing the behavior of certain individuals or groups, the players. Let us consider an example of chess game, the rules provide that the game shall consist of a finite sequence of moves in a specified order, and the nature of each move is prescribed. Moves are of two kinds, namely personal moves and chance moves. A personal move is a choice by one of the players of one of a specified, possibly infinite, set of alternatives. For instance each move in chess is a personal move, the first move is a choice by White of 1 of 20 specified alternatives. The actual decision made in a particular play of a game at a given personal move we shall call the choice at that move. A chance move results in the choice of one of a specified set of alternatives, here the alternative is selected not by one of the players, but by a chance mechanism, with the probabilities with which the mechanism selects the various alternatives specified by the rules of the game.

Let us consider another example of bridge game. The first move in bridge consists of dealing the first card to a specified player. This is a chance move with 52 alternatives, the rules require to that each alternative shall have probability 1/52 of being selected. The actual selection made in a particular play of a game at a given chance move, we shall call the outcome at that move.

1.2 Games and Solutions

A game is a description of strategic interaction that includes the constraints on the actions that the players can take and the players' interests, but does not specify the actions that the players do take. A solution is a systematic description of the outcomes that may emerge in a family of games. Game theory suggests reasonable solutions for classes of games and examines their properties. We study four groups of game theoretic models, indicated by the titles of the four parts of the book: strategic games (Part I), extensive games with and without perfect information (Parts II and III), and coalitional games (Part IV). We now explain some of the dimensions on which this division is based.

1.3 Noncooperative and Cooperative Games

In all game theoretic models the basic entity is a player. A player may be interpreted as an individual or as a group of individuals making a decision. Once we define the set of players, we may distinguish between two types of models: those in which the sets of possible actions of individual players are primitives (Parts I, II, and III) and those in which the sets of possible joint actions of groups of players are primitives (Part IV). Sometimes models of the first type are referred to as "noncooperative", while those of the second type are referred to as "cooperative" (though these terms do not express well the differences between the models). The numbers of pages that we devote to each of these branches of the theory reflect the fact that in recent years most research has been devoted to noncooperative games; it does not express our evaluation of the relative importance of the two branches. In particular, we do not share the view of some authors that noncooperative models are more "basic" than cooperative ones; in our opinion, neither group of models is more "basic" than the other.

1.4 Strategic Games and Extensive Games

In Part I we discuss the concept of a strategic game and in Parts II and III the concept of an extensive game. A strategic game is a model of a situation in which each player chooses his plan of action once and for all, and all players' decisions are made simultaneously (that is, when choosing a plan of action each player is not informed of the plan of action chosen by any other player). By contrast, the model of an extensive game specifies the possible orders of events; each player can consider his plan of action not only at the beginning of the game but also whenever he has to make a decision.

1.5 Games with Perfect and Imperfect Information

The third distinction that we make is between the models in Parts II and III. In the models in Part II the participants are fully informed about each others' moves, while in the models in Part III they may be imperfectly informed. The former models have firmer foundations. The latter were developed intensively only in the 1980s; we put less emphasis on them not because they are less realistic or important but because they are less mature.

1.6 Game Theory and the Theory of Competitive Equilibrium

To clarify further the nature of game theory, we now contrast it with the theory of competitive equilibrium that is used in economics. Game theoretic reasoning takes into account the attempts by each decision-maker to obtain, prior to making his decision, information about the other players' behavior, while competitive reasoning assumes that each agent is interested only in some environmental parameters (such as prices), even though these parameters are determined by the actions of all agents. To illustrate the difference between the theories, consider an environment in which the level of some activity (like fishing) of each agent depends on the level of pollution.

To clarify further the nature of game theory, we now contrast it with the theory of competitive equilibrium that is used in economics. Game theoretic reasoning takes into account the attempts by each decision-maker to obtain, prior to making his decision, information about the other players' behavior, while competitive reasoning assumes that each agent is interested only in some environmental parameters (such as prices), even though these parameters are determined by the actions of all agents. To illustrate the difference between the theories, consider an environment in which the level of some activity (like fishing) of each agent depends on the level of pollution, which in turn depends on the levels of each activities.

1.7 Strategic Games

A strategic game is a model of interactive decision-making in which each decision-maker chooses his plan of action once and for all, and these choices are made simultaneously. The model consists of a finite N set of players and, for each player i, a set Ai of actions and a preference relation on the set of action profiles. We refer to an action profile $a = (a_j)_{\epsilon N}$ as an outcome, and denote the set $X_{j \epsilon N} Aj$ of outcomes by A. The requirement that the preferences of each player i be defined over A, rather than A_i, is the feature that distinguishes a strategic game from a decision problem. Each player may not care about his own action but care about the actions taken by the other players.

Thus we defined a strategic game as follows: A strategic game consists of

> ➤ *a finite set N (the set of players)*
> ➤ *for each player iϵN a nonempty set A_i (the set of actions available to player i)*
> ➤ *for each player i e N a preference relation $\exists$ on $A = x_{j \epsilon N} A_j$ (the preference relation of player i).*

If the set A_i of actions of every player i is finite then the game is finite.

1.8 Analysis of Strategic Game

The high level of abstraction of this model allows it to be applied to a wide variety of situations. A player may be an individual human being or any other decision-making entity like a government, a board of directors, the leadership of a revolutionary movement, or even a flower or an animal. The model places no restrictions on the set of actions available to a player, which may, for example, contain just a few elements or be a huge set containing complicated plans that cover a variety of contingencies. However, the range of application of the model is limited by the requirement that we associate with each player a preference relation. A player's preference relation may simply reflect the player's feelings about the possible outcomes or, in the case of an organism that does not act consciously, the chances of its reproductive success. The fact that the model is so abstract is a merit to the extent that it allows applications in a wide range of situations, but is a drawback to the extent that the implications of the model cannot depend on any specific features of a situation. Indeed, very few conclusions can be reached about the outcome of a game at this level of abstraction; one needs to be much more specific to derive interesting results. In some situations the players' preferences are most naturally defined not over action profiles but over their consequences. When modeling an oligopoly, for example, we may take the set of players to be a set of firms and the set of actions of each firm to be the set of prices; but we may wish to model the assumption that each firm cares only about its profit, not about the profile of prices that generates that profit. To do so we introduce a set C of consequences, a function g: A→C that associates consequences with action profiles, and a profile (∃i*) of preference relations over C. Then the preference relation (∃i) of each player i in the strategic game is defined as follows: a ≡ b if and only if g(a)≡i*g(b). Sometimes we wish to model a situation in which the consequence of an action profile is affected by an exogenous random variable whose realization is not known to the players before they take their actions.

We can model such a situation as a strategic game by introducing a set C of consequences, a probability space Ω, and a function g:AxΩ→C with the interpretation that g(a, w) is the consequence when the action profile is a $\in$ A and the realization of the random variable is w$\in\Omega$. A profile of actions induces a lottery on C; for each player i, a preference relation ∃i* must be specified over the set of all such lotteries. Player i's preference relation in the strategic game is defined as follows: a≡$_i$b if and only if the lottery over C induced by g(a,.) is at least as good according to ≡i* as the lottery induced by g(b,.).

	L	R
T	w1, w2	x1, x2
B	y1, y2	z1, z2

Figure 1.1

Under a wide range of circumstances the preference relation ≡i of player i in a strategic game can be represented by a payoff function. Ui: A→R. (also called a utility function), in the sense that Ui(a) ≥Ui(b) whenever a≡ib. We refer to values of such a function as payoffs (or utilities). Frequently we specify a player's preference relation by giving a payoflf function that represents it. In such a case we denote the game by $(N, (A_i), (U_i))$ rather than $(N, (A_i), (\equiv_i))$.

It is a convenient representation of a two-player strategic game in which each player has two strategies. A finite strategic game in which there are two players can be described conveniently in a table like that in Figure 1.1. One player's actions are identified with the rows and the other player's with the columns. The two numbers in the box formed by row r and column c are the players' payoffs when the row player chooses r and the column player chooses c, the first component being the payoff of the row player. Thus in the game in Figure 1.1 the set of actions of the row player is $\{T, B\}$ and that of the column player is $\{L, R\}$, and for example the row player's payoff from the outcome (T, L) is w_1 and the column player's payoff is w_2. If the players' names are "1" and "2" then the convention is that the row player is player 1 and the column player is player 2.

A common interpretation of a strategic game is that it is a model of an event that occurs only once; each player knows the details of the game and the fact that all the players are "rational", and the players choose their actions simultaneously and independently. Under this interpretation each player is unaware, when choosing his action, of the choices being made by the other players; there is no information (except the primitives of the model) on which a player can base his expectation of the other players' behavior.

When referring to the actions of the players in a strategic game as "simultaneous" we do not necessarily mean that these actions are taken at the same point in time. One situation that can be modeled as a strategic game is the following. The players are at different locations, in front of terminals. First the players' possible actions and payoffs are described publicly (so that they are common knowledge among the players). Then each player chooses an action by sending a message to a central computer; the players are informed of their payoffs when all the messages have been received. However, the model of a strategic game is much more widely applicable than this example suggests. For a situation to be modeled as a strategic game it is important only that the players make decisions independently, no player being informed of the choice of any other player prior to making his own decision.

1.9 Nash Equilibrium

The most commonly used solution concept in game theory is that of Nash equilibrium. This notion captures a steady state of the play of a strategic game in which each player holds the correct expectation about the other players' behavior and acts rationally. It does not attempt to examine the process by which a steady state is reached.

A Nash equilibrium of a strategic game $(N, (Ai),(\equiv i))$ is a profile $a^* \in A$ of actions with the property that for every player $i \in N$ we have

$$(a^*_{-i}, a^*_i) \equiv_i (a^*_{-i}, a_i) \text{ for all } a_i \in A_i.$$

Thus for a^* to be a Nash equilibrium it must be that no player i has an action yielding an outcome that he prefers to that generated when he chooses a^*_i, given that every other player j chooses his equilibrium action a^*_j. Briefly, no player can profitably deviate, given the actions of the other players. The following restatement of the definition is sometimes useful. For any $a_i \in a_{-i}$ define $B_i(a_{-i})$ to be the set of player i's best actions given a_{-i}.

$$B_i(a_{-i}) = \{a_i \in A_i : (a_{-i}, a_i) \gtrsim_i (a_{-i}, a_i') \text{ for all } a_i' \in A_i\} \quad\text{——— (1)}$$

We call the set-valued function B_i the best-response function of player i. A Nash equilibrium is a profile a^* of actions for which

$$a_i^* \in B_i(a_{-i}^*) \text{ for all } i \in N \quad\text{——— (2)}$$

This alternative formulation of the definition points us to a (not necessarily efficient) method of finding Nash equilibria: first calculate the best response function of each player, then find a profile a^* of actions for which $a_i^* \in B_i(a_{-i})$ for all $i \in N$. If the functions B_i are singleton-valued then the second step entails solving $|N|$ equations in the $|N|$ unknowns $(a_{i^*})_{i \in N}$

1.10 Illustrations

The following classical games represent a variety of strategic situations. The games are very simple. In each game there are just two players and each player has only two possible actions. Nevertheless, each game captures the essence of a type of strategic interaction that is frequently present in more complex situations.

Let us consider two people wish to go out together to a concert of music by either Bob or Anan. Their main concern is to go out together, but one person prefers Bob and the other person prefers Anan. Representing the individuals' preferences by payoff functions, we have the game in Figure 1.2. The game has two Nash equilibria: (Bob, Bob) and (Anan, Anan). That is, there are two steady states: one in which both players always choose Bob and one in which they always choose Anan.

	Bob	Anan
Bob	2,1	0,0
Anan	0,0	1,2

Figure 1.2

1.11 Co-Ordination Game

As in Fig-1.2, two people wish to go out together, but in this case they agree on the more desirable concert. A game that captures this situation is given in Figure 1.2. Like Bob and Anan, the game has two Nash equilibria, ie., two people wish to go out together, but in this case they agree on the more desirable concert.

A game that captures this situation is given in Figure 1.3. Like Bob and Anan, the game has two Nash equilibria for the co-ordinate game: (Mom, Mom) and (Pop, Pop). In contrast to Fig.1.3

	Mom	Pop
Mom	2,2	0,0
Pop	0,0	1,1

Figure 1.3

the players have a mutual interest in reaching one of these equilibria, namely (Mom, Mom). However, the notion of Nash equilibrium does not rule out a steady state in which the outcome is the inferior equilibrium (Pop, Pop).

THE PRISONER'S DILEMMA

Two suspects in a crime are put into separate cells. If they both confess, each will be sentenced to three years in prison. If only one of them confesses, he will be freed and used as a witness against the other, who will receive a sentence of four years. If neither confesses, they will both be convicted of a minor offense and spend one year in prison. Choosing a convenient payoff representation for the preferences, we have the game in Figure 1.4. (Confess, Confess).

	Don't Confess	Confess
Don't Confess	3,3	0,4
Confess	4,0	1,1

	Dove	Hawk
Dove	3,3	1,4
Hawk	4,1	0,0

Fig. 1.4

This is a game in which there are gains from cooperation— the best outcome for the players is that neither confesses—but each player has an incentive to be a "free rider". Whatever one player does, the other prefers Confess to Don't Confess, so that the game has a unique Nash equilibrium Example (Dove-Hawk) Two animals are fighting over some prey. Each can behave like a dove or like a hawk. The best outcome for each animal is that in which it acts like a hawk while the other acts like a dove; the worst outcome is that in which both animals act like hawks. Each animal prefers to be hawkish if its opponent is dovish and dovish if its opponent is hawkish. A game that captures this situation is shown in Figure 1.5. The game has two Nash equilibria, (Dove, Hawk) and (Crow, Hawk), corresponding to two different conventions about the player who yields.

2.1 Matching Pennies

Each of two people chooses either Head or Tail. If the choices differ, person 1 pays person 2 a dollar; if they are the same, person 2 pays person 1 a dollar. Each person cares only about the amount of money that he receives. A game that models this situation is shown in Figure 1.6. Such a game, in which the interests of the players are diametrically opposed, is called "strictly competitive". The game Matching Pennies has no Nash equilibrium.

	Head	Tail
Head	1,-1	-1,1
Tail	-1,1	1,-1

Fig. 1.5

The notion of a strategic game encompasses situations much more complex than those described in the last five examples. The following are representatives of three families of games that have been studied extensively: auctions, games of timing, and location games.

2.2 Existence of a Nash Equilibrium

Not every strategic game has a Nash equilibrium, as the game Matching Pennies. The conditions under which the set of Nash equilibria of a game is nonempty have been investigated extensively. We now present an existence result that is one of the simplest of the genre. An existence result has two purposes. First, if we have a game that satisfies the hypothesis of the result then we know that there is some hope that our efforts to find an equilibrium will meet with success. Second, and more important, the existence of an equilibrium shows that the game is consistent with a steady state solution. Further, the existence of equilibria for a family of games allows us to study properties of these equilibria (by using, for example, "comparative static" techniques) without finding them explicitly and without taking the risk that we are studying the empty set. To show that a game has a Nash equilibrium it suffices to show that there is a profile a* of actions such that a* G B^a*^) for all i G N). Define the set-valued function B:A -> A by B(a) = XjejvBj(a_i). Equation can be written in vector form simply as a* G B(a*). Fixed point theorems give conditions on B under which there indeed exists a value of a* for which a* G B(a*).

A general model of an extensive game allows each player, when making his choices, to be imperfectly informed about what has happened in the past. In this part we investigate a simpler model in which each player is perfectly informed about the players' previous actions at each point in the game.

2.3 Definition of Extensive Game

An extensive game is a detailed description of the sequential structure of the decision problems encountered by the players in a strategic situation. There is perfect information in such a game if each player, when making any decision, is perfectly informed of all the events that have previously occurred. For simplicity we initially restrict attention to games in which no two players make decisions at the same time and all relevant moves are made by the players (no randomness ever intervenes).

An extensive game with perfect information has the following components:

> A set N (the set of players).
> A set H of sequences (finite or infinite) that satisfies the following three properties.
> The empty sequence φ is a member of H.
> If $(a^k)_{k=1,\ldots,K} \in H$ (where K may be infinite) and $L < K$ then $(a^k)_{k=1,\ldots,L} \in H$

If an infinite sequence $(a^k)_{k=1,\ldots,}$ satisfies $a^k)_{k=1,\ldots,L} \in H$ for every positive integer L then $a^k)_{k=1,\ldots} \in H$.

(Each member of H is a history; each component of a history is an action taken by a player.) $(a^k)_{k=1,\ldots,K} \in H$ is terminal if it is infinite or if there is no a^{K+1} such that $((a^k)_{k=1,\ldots,K+1} +i \in H$.

The set of terminal histories is denoted Z.*

> A function P that assigns to each nonterminal history (each member of H \ Z) a member of N. (P is the player function, P(h) being the player who takes an action after the history h.)

➤ For each player i $\in$N a preference relation $>_i$ on Z (the preference relation of player i).

Sometimes it is convenient to specify the structure of an extensive game without specifying the players' preferences. We refer to a triple (N, H, P) whose components satisfy the first three conditions in the definition as an extensive game form with perfect information.

If the set H of possible histories is finite then the game is finite. If the length of every history is finite then the game has a finite horizon. Let h be a history of length k; we denote by (h, a) the history of length k+1 consisting of h followed by a.

Throughout this chapter we refer to an extensive game with perfect information simply as an "extensive game". We interpret such a game as follows. After any non terminal history h player P(h) chooses an action from the set A(h) = {a:(h,a)$\in$H}. The empty history is the starting point of the game; we sometimes refer to it as the initial history. At this point player P(φ) chooses a member of A(φ). For each possible choice a^0 from this set player P(a°) subsequently chooses a member of the set A(a°); this choice determines the next player to move, and so on. A history after which no more choices have to be made is terminal. Note that a history may be an infinite sequence of actions. Implicit in the definition of a history as a sequence (rather than as a more complex mathematical object, like a string of sequences) is the assumption that no action may be taken after any infinite history, so that each such history is terminal. As in the case of a strategic game we often specify the players' preferences over terminal histories by giving payoff functions that represent the preferences.

Example:

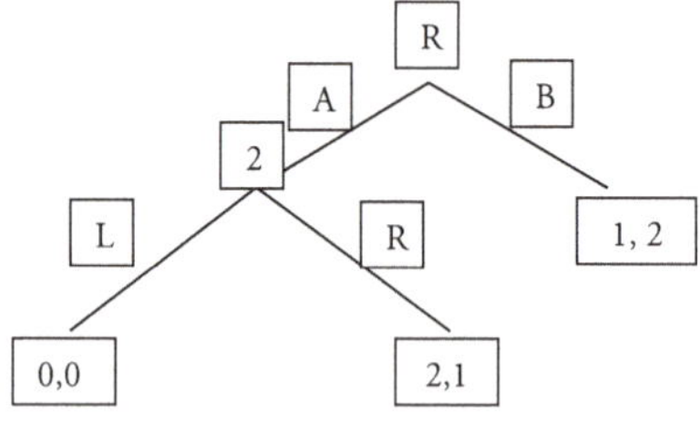

The game in above Figure has two Nash equilibria: (A, R) and (B, L), with payoff profiles (2,1) and (1,2). The strategy profile (B, L) is a Nash equilibrium because given that player 2 chooses L after the history A, it is optimal for player 1 to choose B at the start of the game (if she chooses A instead, then given player 2's choice she obtains 0 rather than 1), and given player 1's choice of B it is optimal for player 2 to choose L (since his choice makes no difference to the outcome).

2.4 Subgame Perfect Equilibrium

Definition: The subgame of the extensive game with perfect information F = (N, H, P, (>$_i$)) that follows the history h is the extensive game F(h) = (N, H\h, P\htQZi\h)) i where H\h is the set of sequences h' of actions for which (h, h') ∈ H, P|/, is defined by P\h(h') = P(h, h') for each h' e H\h, and £4 is defined by h' £4 h" if and only if (h, h') £4 (h, h"). The notion of equilibrium we now define requires that the action prescribed by each player's strategy be optimal, given the other players' strategies, after every history. Given a strategy s^ of player i and a history h in the extensive game F, denote by Si\h the strategy that Sj induces in the subgame F(h) (i.e. s,|/,(^') = Si(h, h') for each h' e H\h); denote by Oh the outcome function of T(h).

2.5 Bargaining Game Theory

Game theory deals with situations in which people's interests conflict. The people involved may try to resolve the conflict by committing themselves voluntarily to a course of action that is beneficial to all of them. If there is more than one course of action more desirable than disagreement for all individuals and there is conflict over which course of action to pursue then some form of negotiation over how to resolve the conflict is necessary. The negotiation process may be modeled using the tools of game theory; the model in this chapter is an example of such an analysis. Since the presence of a conflict of interest is central to game theoretic situations, the theory of bargaining is more than just an application of game theory; models of bargaining lie at the heart of the subject and have attracted a great deal of attention since its inception. We use the model of an extensive game with perfect information to study some features of bargaining, in particular the influence of the participants' impatience and the risk aversion on the outcome.

2.6 A Bargaining Game of Alternating Offers

Consider a situation in which two bargainers have the opportunity to reach agreement on an outcome in some set X and perceive that if they fail to do so then the outcome will be some fixed event D. The set X may, for example, be the set of feasible divisions of a desirable pie and D may be the event in which neither party receives any of the pie. To model such a situation as an extensive game we have to specify the procedure that the parties follow when negotiating. The procedure we study is one in which the players alternate offers. It can be described conveniently by introducing the variable "time", the values of which are the nonnegative integers. The first move of the game occurs in period 0, when player 1 makes a proposal (a member of X), which player 2 then either accepts or rejects. Acceptance ends the game while rejection leads to period 1, in which player 2 makes a proposal, which player 1 has to accept or reject. Again, acceptance ends the game; rejection leads to period 2, in which it is once again player 1's turn to make a proposal. The game continues in this fashion: so long as no offer has been accepted, in every even period player 1 makes a proposal that player 2 must either accept or reject, and in every odd period player 2 makes a proposal that player 1 must either accept or reject. There is no bound on the number of rounds of negotiation: the game has an infinite horizon. The fact that some offer is rejected places no restrictions on the offers that may subsequently be made. In particular, a player who rejects a proposal x may subsequently make a proposal that is worse for him than x. If no offer is ever accepted then the outcome is the disagreement event D. We now give a formal description of the situation as an extensive game with perfect information. The set of players is N = {1, 2}. Let X, the set of possible agreements, be a compact connected subset of a Euclidian space, and let T be the set of nonnegative integers. The set of histories H is the set of all sequences of one of the following types, where t $\in$ T, x' $\in$ X for all s, A means "accept", and R means "reject".

   I.   φ **(the initial history), or** $(x^0, R, x^1, R,..., x^t, R)$

   II. $(x^0, R, x^1, R,..., x^t)$

   III. $(x^0, R, x^1, R,..., x^t, A)$

   IV. $(x^0, R, x^1, R,...)$

It follows from this description of the histories that the player whose turn it is to move chooses a member of X after a history of type I and a member of {A, R} after a history of type II. Histories of type III and IV are terminal; those of type III are finite, while those of type IV are infinite. The player function is defined as follows: $P(h) = 1$ if h is of type I or type II and t is odd or if h is empty; $P(h) = 2$ if h is of type I or type II and t is even. To complete the description of the game we need to specify the players' preferences over terminal histories. We assume that each player cares only about whether agreement is reached and the time and content of the agreement, not about the path of proposals that preceded the agreement. Precisely, the set of terminal histories is partitioned as follows: for each $x \in X$ and $t \in T$ the set of all histories of type III for which $z^* = x$ is a member of the partition, denoted by $(*, t)$, and the set of all histories of type IV is a member of the partition, denoted by D. The preference relation of each player i over histories is induced from a preference relation $\pounds<$ over the set $(X \times T) \cup \{D\}$ of members of this partition.

2.7 Repeated Games

The model of a repeated game is designed to examine the logic of longterm interaction. It captures the idea that a player will take into account the effect of his current behavior on the other players' future behavior, and aims to explain phenomena like cooperation, revenge, and threats.

	C	D
C	3,3	0,4
D	4,0	1,1

Figure 2.1

The basic idea behind the theory is illustrated by the case in which two individuals repeatedly play the Prisoner's Dilemma. This game has a unique Nash equilibrium, in which each player chooses D; further, for each player the action D strictly dominates the action C, so that the rationale behind the outcome (D, D) is very strong. Despite this, both players are better off if they "cooperate" and choose C. The main idea behind the theory of repeated games is that if the game is played repeatedly then the mutually desirable outcome in which (C, C) occurs in every period is stable if each player believes that a defection will terminate the cooperation, resulting in a subsequent loss for him that outweighs the short-term gain. The primary achievement of the theory is to isolate types of strategies that support mutually desirable outcomes in any game. The theory gives us insights into the structure of behavior when individuals interact repeatedly, structure that may be interpreted in terms of a "social norm". The results that we describe show that the social norm needed to sustain mutually desirable outcomes involves each player's "punishing" any player whose behavior is undesirable. When we impose the requirement embedded in the notion of subgame perfect equilibrium that threats of punishment be credible, the social norm must also ensure that the punishers have an incentive to carry out the threats in circumstances in which the social norm requires them to do so. In this case the precise nature of the punishment depends on how the players value future outcomes. Sometimes it is sufficient that a punishment phase last for a limited amount of time, after which the players return to pursue the mutually desirable outcome; sometimes the social norm must entail future rewards for players who can out costly punishments Although we regard these results about the structure of the equilibrium strategies to be the main achievement of the theory, most of the results in the literature focus instead on the set of payoffs that can be sustained by equilibria, giving conditions under which this set consists of nearly all reasonable payoff profiles. These "folk theorems" have two sides.

On the one hand they demonstrate that socially desirable outcomes that cannot be sustained if players are short-sighted can be sustained if the players have long-term objectives. On the other hand they show that the set of equilibrium outcomes of a repeated game is huge, so that the notion of equilibrium lacks predictive power. "Folk theorems" are the focus of much of the formal development in this chapter. Nevertheless, we stress that in our opinion the main contribution of the theory is the discovery of interesting stable social norms (strategies) that support mutually desirable payoff profiles, and not simply the demonstration that equilibria exist that generate such profiles.

Chapter 3

INFINITELY REPEATED GAMES VS. FINITELY REPEATED GAMES

The model of a repeated game has two versions: the horizon may be finite or infinite. As we shall see, the results in the two cases are different. An extreme (and far from general) case of the difference is that in which the constituent game is the Prisoner's Dilemma. We shall see below that in any finite repetition of this game the only Nash equilibrium outcome is that in which the players choose {D, D) in every period on the other hand, in the infinitely repeated game the set of subgame perfect equilibrium payoff profiles is huge. Thus in applying the model of a repeated game in specific situations we may need to determine whether a finite or infinite horizon is appropriate.

3.1 Comparison with Prisoner's Dilemma

In our view a model should attempt to capture the features of reality that the players perceive; it should not necessarily aim to describe the reality that an outside observer perceives, though obviously there are links between the two perceptions. Thus the fact that a situation has a horizon that is in some physical sense finite (or infinite) does not necessarily imply that the best model of the situation has a finite (or infinite) horizon. A model with an infinite horizon is appropriate if after each period the players believe that the game will continue for an additional period, while a model with a finite horizon is appropriate if the players clearly perceive a well-defined final period. The fact that players have finite lives, for example, does not imply that one should always model their strategic interaction as a finitely repeated game. If they play a game so frequently that the horizon approaches only very slowly then they may ignore the existence of the horizon entirely until its arrival is imminent, and until this point their strategic thinking may be better captured by a game with an infinite horizon. In a situation that is objectively finite, a key criterion that determines whether we should use a model with a finite or an infinite horizon is whether the last period enters explicitly into the players' strategic considerations. For this reason, even some situations that involve a small number of repetitions are better analyzed as infinitely repeated games. For example, when laboratory subjects are instructed to play the Prisoner's Dilemma twenty times with payoffs as in Figure2.1 above (interpreted as dollars), I believe that their lines of reasoning are better modeled by an infinitely repeated game than by a 20-period repeated game, since except very close to the end of the game they are likely to ignore the existence of the final period.

The behavior of experimental subjects who play the Prisoner's Dilemma repeatedly a finite number of times is inconsistent with the unique subgame perfect equilibrium of the finitely repeated game. The fact that it may be consistent with some subgame perfect equilibrium of the infinitely repeated game is uninteresting since the range of outcomes that are so-consistent is vast. Certainly the subgame perfect equilibria of the infinitely repeated game give no insights about the dependence of the subjects' behavior on the magnitude of the payoffs and the length of the game The experimental results definitely indicate that the notion of subgame perfect equilibrium in the finitely repeated Prisoner's Dilemma does not capture human behavior. However, this deficiency appears to have more to do with the backwards induction inherent in the notion of subgame perfect equilibrium than with the finiteness of the horizon.

A model that will give us an understanding of the facts is likely to be a variant of the finitely repeated game; some characteristics of the equilibria of the infinitely repeated game may be suggestive, but this model itself appears unpromising as an explanatory tool. Moreover, in contexts in which the constituent game has multiple Nash equilibria, the equilibria of finitely repeated games correspond well with the casual observation that people act cooperatively when the horizon is distant and opportunistically when it is near; the equilibria of infinitely repeated games can give us no insight into such behavior. Finally, in situations in which people's discount factors decline to zero over time, even if they never become zero (i.e. no fixed finite horizon is perceived), the equilibrium outcomes have more in common with those of finitely repeated games than with those of infinitely repeated games.

In much of the existing literature the fact that the set of equilibria in a long finitely repeated game may be very different from the set of equilibria of an infinite repetition of the same constituent game is regarded as "disturbing". In contrast, we find it attractive: the two models capture a very realistic feature of life, namely the fact that the existence of a prespecified finite period may crucially affect people's behavior (consider the last few months of a presidency or the fact that religions attempt to persuade their believers that there is "life after death").

First, for a large set of constituent games there is no discontinuity between the outcomes of the associated finitely and infinitely repeated games. Second, in some cases in which the discontinuity does exist it is indeed unappealing. If people who are faced with a known fixed distant horizon behave as if the horizon is infinite then this should be the prediction of a model with a fixed finite horizon; if it is not then doubts are raised about the plausibility of the notion of subgame perfect equilibrium in other contexts.

3.2 Infinitely Repeated Games: Definitions

The model of an infinitely repeated game captures a situation in which players repeatedly engage in a strategic game G, which we refer to as the constituent game. Throughout we restrict attention to games in which played; on each occasion the players choose their actions simultaneously. When taking an action, a player knows the actions previously chosen by all players. We model this situation as an extensive game with perfect information (and simultaneous moves) as follows.

Definition

Let $G = (N, (Ai), (>_i, \bullet))$ be a strategic game; let $A = X_{i \in N} \in A_i$

An infinitely repeated game of G is an extensive game with perfect information and simultaneous moves $(N, H, P, (>_i, \bullet))$ in which

> $H = U_{t=0\ldots\infty} A^*$ (where $A^0 = \{\varphi\}$ is the initial history)
> $P(h) = N$ for each nonterminal history $h \in H$
> $(>_i, \bullet)$ is a preference relation on the set A^∞ of infinite sequences $(a^t)^0_{t=0\ldots\infty}$ of action profiles in G that extends the $(>_i,)$ preference relation in the sense that it satisfies the following condition of weak separability: if $(a^t) \in A^\infty$, $a \in A$, $a' \in A$, and $a >_i a'$ then

$$(a^1,\ldots,a^t,a,a^{t+1}\ldots) >_i (a^1,\ldots,a^t,a',a^{t+1}\ldots) \text{ for all values of } t.$$

A history is terminal if and only if it is infinite. After any nonterminal history every player $i \in N$ chooses an action in Ai. Thus a strategy of player t is a function that assigns an action in Ai to every finite sequence of outcomes in G. We now impose restrictions on the players' preference relations in addition to weak separability. We assume throughout that player t's preference relation $>_i$ in the repeated game is based upon a payoff function Uj that represents his preference relation $>_i$ in G: we assume that whether $a^t >_i b^t$ depends only on the relation between the corresponding sequences $(u_i(a^t))$ and $(u_i(b^t))$ of payoffs in G.

We consider three forms of the preference relations, the first of which is defined as follows.

> *Discounting: There is some number $\delta \in (0,1)$ (the discount factor) such that the sequence (v_i^t) of real numbers is at least as good as the sequence (w_i^t) if and only if $\sum t=0\ldots\infty$ $\delta^t(v_i^t - w_i^t) > 0$.*

3.3 Discounting criterion with Pay-offs

Under the discounting criterion a change in the payoff in a single period can matter, whereas under the limit of means criterion payoff differences in any finite number of periods do not matter. A player whose preferences satisfy the limit of means is ready to sacrifice any loss in the first finite number of periods in order to increase the stream of payoffs he eventually obtains. For example, the stream $(0,...,0,2,2,...)$ of payoffs is preferred by the limit of means criterion to the constant stream $(1,1,...)$ independent of the index of the period in which the player first gets 2 in the first stream. At first sight this property may seem strange. However, it is not difficult to think of situations in which decision makers put overwhelming emphasis on the long run at the expense of the short run (think of nationalist struggles).

We now introduce a criterion that treats all periods symmetrically and puts emphasis on the long run but at the same time is sensitive to a change in payoff in a single period. (Again we define the criterion in terms of the strict preference relation.) Similarly we define the limit of means infinitely repeated game of $(N, (Ai), (ui))$ and the overtaking infinitely repeated game of $(N,(Ai),(ui))$. We denote by $u(a)$ the profile $Ui(a)i \in N$. Define a vector $v \in R^N$ to be a payoff profile of $(N, (Ai), (u_i))$ if there is an outcome $a \in A$ for which $v = u(a)$. We refer to a vector $v \in R^N$ as a feasible payoff profile of $(N, (Ai, (ui))$ if it is a convex combination of payoff profiles of outcomes in A.

To illuminate the character of equilibria in which each player uses a trigger strategy, consider two infinitely repeated games: one in which the constituent game is the Prisoner's

Dilemma, which we denote G1 (Figure 2.1), and the other in which the constituent game is the game G2 shown in Figure2.2.

	A	D
C	2,3	1,5
D	0,1	0,1

Figure 2.2

In both G1 and G2 each player's minmax payoff is 1 and by playing D each player holds the other's payoff to this level ($p\_1 = p\_2 = D$). In both games the trigger strategies used in the proof of proposition involve each player switching to D for good in response to any deviation from the equilibrium path. In Gi the action D dominates the action C, so that it is a stable order for each player to choose D. Thus there is some rationale for a punisher who believes that a deviation signals the end of the current stable order to choose the action D in the future. By contrast, in G2 a constant repetition of (D, D) is not a stable order since A strictly dominates D for player 1. The strategies used in the proof of proposition to generate an arbitrary enforceable payoff profile punish a deviant indefinitely. Such punishment is unnecessarily harsh: a deviant's payoff needs to be held down to the minmax level only for enough periods to wipe out his (one-period) gain from the deviation. If the players' preferences satisfy the limit of means criterion then a strategy that returns to the equilibrium path after the punishment, has the advantage that it yields the same payoff for the punishers as does the equilibrium path itself, so that the players have no reason not to adopt it. Hence under the limit of means criterion the social norm of punishing for only a finite number of periods is a subgame perfect equilibrium of the infinitely repeated game.

The strategies that we define in this proof do not initiate punishment immediately after a deviation, but wait until the end of a cycle before doing so. We define the strategies in this way in order to calculate easily the length of punishment, necessary to deter a deviation: if punishment were to begin immediately after a deviation then we would have to take into account, when we calculated the length of the required punishment, the possibility that a deviant's payoffs in the remainder of the cycle are low, so that he has an additional gain from terminating the cycle.

The intuitive argument that drives the folk theorems for infinitely repeated games is that a mutually desirable outcome can be supported by a stable social arrangement in which a player is deterred from deviating by the threat that he will be "punished" if he does so. The same argument applies, with modifications, to a large class of finitely repeated games. The need for modification is rooted in the fact that the outcome in the last period of any Nash equilibrium of any finitely repeated game must be a Nash equilibrium of the constituent game, a fact that casts a shadow over the rest of the game. This shadow is longest in the special case in which every player's payoff in every Nash equilibrium of the constituent game is equal to his minmax payoff (as in the Prisoner's Dilemma). In this case the intuitive argument behind the folk theorems fails: the outcome in every period must be a Nash equilibrium of the constituent game, since if there were a period in which the outcome were not such an equilibrium then in the last such period some player could deviate with impurity.

Chapter 4

INTRODUCTION ON NETWORK APPLICATIONS

Traditionally the network design is based on developing a set of general rules. These rules worked well when there were not too many choices in technologies, interconnection strategies, routing protocols and so on. The network design focused primarily on capacity planning. The capacity planning is still an important part of the design process, we now also need to consider how we can optimize delay in the network. In many cases, reliability means much more than redundant paths in the network or resilient routing protocols.

4.1 Network Services

The network services are defined as levels of performance and function that are offered y the network, host, and/or application, to the rest of the system, or as sets of requirements that are expected from the network by the end user, application, or host. Levels of performance will be described by performance characteristics such as capacity, delay and reliability, while the functions include security, accounting, billing, scheduling and management. The network services are applied by grouping network performance and functional characteristics together and using these characteristics to configure, monitor and verify the service in the network.

Service characteristics and requirements are useful in the network analysis and design processes from two perspectives. That is in configuring services in network elements and providing input into the network design. The services characteristics such as individual network performance and functional parameters are used to describe services that are offered by the network to the system or that are requested from the network by users, applications, or hosts. The service characteristics used to configure services in network, and as service metrics to measure and verify services. Services need to be configurable, measurable and verifiable within the system. It is necessary to insure that the end users are getting the services they are requesting (and probably paying for) and leads to accounting and billing for system including network, resources.

The service requirements or characteristics are groped together to describe service levels for the network. The service levels are helpful in service accounting and billing. There are many ways to describe service levels, including Committed Information Rates (CIRs), Classes of Service (COSs), Types of Service (TOSs), Quality of Service(QOSs) and custom service levels based on groups of individual service characteristics depending on which network technology, protocol or combination of these is providing the service.

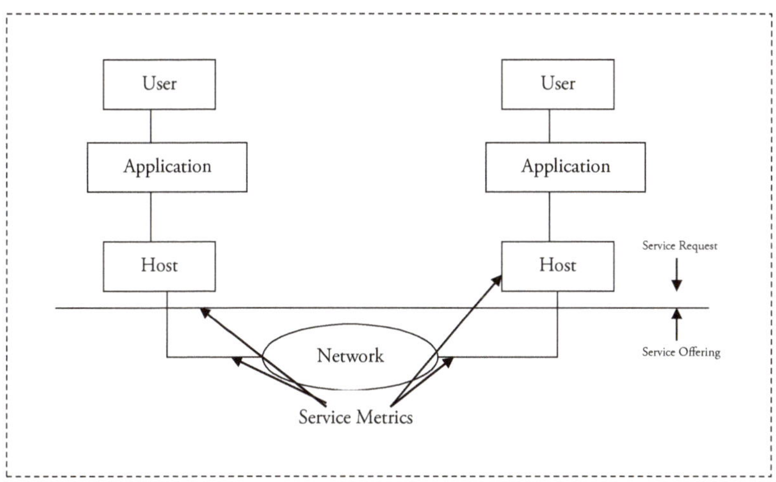

Figure – 4.1

4.1.1 Service level demarcation

The Figure 4.1 indicates where service offerings, service requests and service metrics are applied in the system. In the above figure, the demarcation of services is shown between the host and network components. Depending on the service requirement or characteristics, however, the demarcation may also be between the host and application components. Services and service levels can be distinguished by their degrees of predictability or determinism, and by their degrees of performance. The service performance characteristics in terms of reliability (i.e., availability),capacity (ie., bandwidth) and delay (i.e., latency) are used to describe services and service levels.

4.2 Characterizing services

One of the major goals of network analysis is to be able to characterize services so that they can be designed into the network and requested from vendors and service providers.

In addition to today's best effort delivery services, we will examine new types of services, specified services as well as high and low performance services.

4.2.1 Service Requests

Service requests are distinguished by the degree of predictability needed in the service. Based on predictability, service requests are placed into best-effort and specified groups. The best-effort service means that there is no control over how the network will satisfy the service request, that no guarantees are presented nor is the network obligated to do more than try. Such requests indicate that the rest f the system (user, application, and host) will need to adapt to the state of the network a any given time. Thus the expected service for such requests will be unpredictable and variable across the range of performance values. Such service requests either have no performance requirements for the network, or the requirements are non-specific.

Specified service requests can also be based on the ability to actually guarantee the service through the network. This type of service has the most stringent service requirements and requires a mechanism (such as a service contract and policing) to guarantee service end to end within the system, even to the exclusion of other users, applications, or hosts.

The service performance requirements are described in terms of the service characteristics such as reliability, delay and capacity while service functional requirements are in terms of specific functions such as the need for multicast, security or accounting. Service performance requirement are usually grouped into service levels. Service levels can be the same as specified service requests, but can also be closely related to well-known service offerings from the network, such as ATM QOS or Switched Multimegabit Data Service (SMDS) classes of service. Thus service levels are a way to group service performance requirements into a specified service request that can be mapped onto a well-known or standard network service offering.

4.2.2 Service Offerings

The services offerings are the network counterparts to the service requests from the users, applications and hosts. Like service requests, service offerings are also classified into two groups namely, best-efforts and specified. Best-effort service offerings are not predictable and they are based on the state of the network and there is not control over the network at any time. Most networks today operate in a best-effort mode. The best-effort offering is compatible with the best-effort service request. An example of best-effort service request and offering is when a File Transfer (via FTP) occurs over a best-effort network such as the Internet. FTP uses the Transmission Control Protocol (TCP) as its transport method, which, via a sliding-window flow-control mechanism, adapts to the current state of the network it is operating over. Thus, the service requirement form FTP over TCP is best-effort and the corresponding service offering from the Internet is best-effort. The result is that, while the FTP session is active, the performance characteristics of the network (Internet) and transport method (TCP) are constantly interacting and adapting, as well as contending with other application sessions for network resources. As part of its best-effort service, TCP provides error-free, reliable transmission to the application. Here the service performance requirements reliability, delay and capacity are translated into service performance characteristics. Let us Look at the service performance requirements. It describes the reliability, capacity, throughput and delay

4.2.3 Reliability

Reliability is a measure of the system's ability to provide deterministic and accurate delivery of information. Reliability consists of determinism and accuracy. Reliability can be deterministic in that a guarantee of delivery of information may need to occur within a well-known time boundary. Such a time boundary is composed of an overall completion time for the task as well as a degree of constancy in the time boundary. These time boundaries are set by the system components, such as in TCP or SMTP time-out values, or by the user's perception of reliability.

Reliability requires accuracy in that the information received at the destination must usually be guaranteed to be exactly the same as that sent from the source. This also has a delay component, for the guarantee of accuracy will require error checking and retransmission of lost or error information.

4.2.4 Capacity

Capacity is a measure of the system's ability to transfer information. There are several terms that are often used interchangeably with capacity, such as bandwidth, throughput.

Bandwidth: It is the theoretical capacity of one or more elements or components in the system. Theoretical or raw, bandwidth does not take into account overhead from higher-layer protocols or the performance loss due to inefficiencies in the system.

Throughput: It is the realizable capacity of the system or its components or elements. Values for actual capacity will vary, depending on the system design, types and configuration of equipment and where in the protocol stack the measurement for capacity is being taken.

4.2.5 Delay

Delay is a measure of the time differences in the transmission of information across the system. In its most basic sense, delay is the time difference in transmitting a single unit of information (bit, byte, cell, frame, and packet) from source to destination. This will include delays at various layers, such as propagation, transmission, queueing and processing delays. Both end-to-end and round-trip time measurements are useful with round-trip times measurements are useful, with round-trip times being practical measures of delay, as in the use of ping application. Another measure of delay incorporates application processing and task completion times. As the size of the task increases, the application processing and task completion times also increase. At some point this overall delay; here termed latency may yield important information about the behavior of the applications and the network. Together both delay and latency helps to describe the network behavior.

Chapter 5

EXTENSIVE GAMES WITH IMPERFECT INFORMATION

In this chapter we explore the concept of an extensive game with imperfect information, in which each player, when taking an action, may have only partial information about the actions taken previously.

5.1 Introduction on Extensive Games

In each of the models we studied previously there is a sense in which the players are not perfectly informed when making their choices. In a strategic game a player, when taking an action, does not know the actions that the other players take. In a Bayesian game a player knows neither the other players' private information nor the actions that they take. In an extensive game with perfect information a player does not know the future moves planned by the other players.

The model that we study here an extensive game with imperfect information—differs in that the players may in addition be imperfectly informed about some (or all) of the choices that have already been made. We analyze the model by assuming, as we did previously, that each player, when choosing an action, forms an expectation about the unknowns. However, these expectations differ from those we considered before. Unlike those in strategic games, they are not derived solely from the players' equilibrium behavior, since the players may face situations inconsistent with that behavior. Unlike those in Bayesian games, they are not deduced solely from the equilibrium behavior and the exogenous information about the moves of chance. Finally, unlike those in extensive games with perfect information, they relate not only to the other players' future behavior but Games with Imperfect Information also to events that happened in the past.

The following definition generalizes that of an extensive game with perfect information to allow players to be imperfectly informed about past events when taking actions. It also allows for exogenous uncertainty: some moves may be made by "chance". It does not incorporate the other generalization of the definition of an extensive game with perfect information in which more than one player may move after any history.

Definition: An extensive game has the following components.

- ➢ A finite set N (the set of players).
- ➢ A set H of sequences (finite or infinite) that satisfies the following three properties.
- ➢ The empty sequence 0 is a member of H.
- ➢ If $(a^k)k=i,...,K$ £ H (where K may be infinite) and L < K then

$$(a^k)k=i,...'L \text{ € } H.$$

> ➤ If an infinite sequence $(a^k)k=i,...$ satisfies $(a^k)k=i,...,L$
> € H for every positive integer L then $(a^k)k=i,... $ € H.

(Each member of H is a history; each component of a history is an action taken by a player.) A history $(a^k)k=i,...,K$ € if is terminal and if it is infinite or if there is no a^{K+l} such that (a^k) $k=1,...,k+1$€ H.

The set of actions available after the nonterminal history h is denoted A(h) = {a: (h, a) € H} and the set of terminal histories is denoted Z.

A function P that assigns to each nonterminal history (each member of H \ Z) a member of N U {c}. (P is the player function, P(h) being the player who takes an action after the history h. If P(h) = c then chance determines the action taken after the history h.)

A function fc that associates with every history h for which P(h) = c, a probability measure fc(-\h) on A(h), where each such probability measure is independent of every other such measure. (fc(a\h) is the probability that a occurs after the history h.)

For each player i € N a preference relation £i on lotteries over Z (the preference relation of player i) that can be represented as theexpected value of a payoff function defined on Z. We refer to a tuple (N,H,P,fc,(Ii)ieN) (which excludes the players' preferences) whose components satisfy the conditions in the definition as an extensive game form.

Relative to the definition of an extensive game with perfect information and chance moves, the new element is the collection (Xi)<iN of information partitions. We interpret the histories in any given member of Ij to be indistinguishable to

player i. Thus the game models a situation in which after any history h € I, € Ij player t is informed that some history in 74 has occurred but is not informed that the history h has occurred. The condition that A(h) = A(h') whenever h and h' are in the same member of Ij captures the idea that if A(h) ^ A(h') then player i could deduce, when he faced A(h), that the history was not h', contrary to our interpretation of Ij. Each player's information partition is a primitive of the game and a player can distinguish between histories in different members of his partition without having to make any inferences from the actions that he observes. As the game is played, a participant may be able, given his conjectures about the other players' behavior, to make inferences that refine this information. Suppose, for example, that the first move of a game is made by player 1, who chooses between a and b, and the second move is made by player 2, one of whose information sets is {a,b}. We interpret this game to model a situation in which player 2 does not observe the choice of player 1: when making his move, he is not informed whether player 1 chose a or b. Nevertheless, when making his move player 2 may infer (from his knowledge of a steady state or from introspection about player 1) that the history is a, even though he does not observe the action chosen by player 1.

Each player's preference relation is defined over lotteries on the set of terminal histories, since even if the players' actions are deterministic the chance moves that the model allows induce such lotteries.

In general, we do not allow more than one player to move after any history. However, there is a sense in which an extensive game as we have defined it can model such a situation. To see this, consider the example above. After player 1 chooses L, the situation in which players 1 and 2 are involved is essentially the same as that captured by a game with perfect information in which they choose actions simultaneously. (This is the reason that in much of the literature the definition of anextensive game with perfect information does not include the possibility of simultaneous moves.) A player's strategy in an extensive game with perfect information is a function that specifies an action for every history after which the player chooses an action.

5.2 Pure strategy

A pure strategy of player i e N in an extensive game (N, H, P, fc, (Ij), (£i)) is a function that assigns an action in A(Ii) to each information set U € Xi. As for an extensive game with perfect information, we can associate with any extensive game a strategic game; see the definitions of the strategic form and reduced strategic form. Note that the outcome of a strategy profile here may be a lottery over the terminal histories, since we allow moves of chance.

5.3 Perfect and Imperfect Recall

The model of an extensive game is capable of capturing a wide range of informational environments. In particular, it can capture situations in which at some points players forget what they knew earlier. We refer to games in which at every point every player remembers whatever he knew in the past as games with perfect recall. To define such games formally, let

{N, H, P, fc, (Xj)) be an extensive game form and let $X_i(h)$ be the record of player i's experience along the history h: $X_i(h)$ is the sequence consisting of the information sets that the player encounters in the history h and the actions that he takes at them, in the order that these events occur.

Definition: An extensive game form has perfect recall if for each player i we have $X_i(h) = X_i(h')$ whenever the histories h and h' are in the same information set of player i. In the left-hand game a player does not know if she has made a choice or not: when choosing an action she does not know whether she is at the beginning of the game or has already chosen her left-hand action. In the middle game the player forgets something that she previously knew: when making a choice at her last information set she is not informed of the action of chance, though she was so informed when she made her previous choice.

In the right-hand game she does not remember the action she took in the past. The literature on games with imperfect recall is very small. In the underlying repeated game that a machine game models, each player, when taking an action, is not informed of past events, including his own previous actions. The size of his memory depends on the structure of his machine. More memory requires more states; since states are costly, even in equilibrium a player still may imperfectly recall his own past actions.

5.4 Principles for the Equivalence of Extensive Games

Some extensive games appear to represent the same strategic situation as others. Consider, for example, the two one-player games in In these games, as in the others in this section, we associate letters with terminal histories. If two terminal histories are assigned the same letter then the two histories represent the same event; in particular, all the players are indifferent between them. Formally, the two games are different: in the left-hand game player 1 makes two decisions, while in the right-hand game she makes only one. However, principles of rationality suggest that the two games model the same situation. We now give further examples of pairs of games that arguably represent the same situation and discuss some principles that generalize these examples. We do not argue that these principles should be taken as axioms; we simply believe that studying them illuminates the meaning of an extensive game, especially one with imperfect information.

The four principles that we consider all preserve the reduced strategic form of the game: if one extensive game is equivalent to another according to the principles then the reduced strategic forms of the two games are the same. Thus a solution concept that does not depend solely on the reduced strategic form may assign different outcomes to games that are equivalent according to the principles; to justify such a solution concept one has to argue that at least one of the principles is inappropriate.

Let Fi be the game and the principles that we discuss claim that this game is equivalent to four other extensive games, as follows. Inflation-Deflation According to this principle Fi is equivalent to the game F2. In F2 player 1 has imperfect recall: at her second information set she is not informed whether she chose r or I at the start of the game. That is, the three histories I, (r,£), and (r,r) are all in the same information set in F2, while in Fj the history I lies in one information set and the histories (r, £) and (r, r) lie in another.

The interpretation that we have given to a game like F2 is that player 1, when acting at the end of the game, has forgotten the action she took at the beginning of the game. However, another interpretation of an information set is that it represents the information about history that is inherent in the structure of the game, information that may be refined by inferences that the players may make.

Under this interpretation a player always remembers what he knew and did in the past and may obtain information by making inferences from this knowledge. Indeed, the argument that Fi and F2 are equivalent relies on the assumption that player 1 is capable of making such inferences. The fact that she is informed whether the history was t or a member of {(r, £), (r, r)} is irrelevant to her strategic calculations, according to the argument, since in any case she can infer this information from her knowledge of her action at the start of the game. Under this interpretation it is inappropriate to refer to a game like "imperfect recall": the information sets reflect imperfections in the information inherent in the situation that can be overridden by the players' abilities to remember their past experience. Formally, according to the inflation-deflation principle the extensive game F is equivalent to the extensive game F' if F' differs from F only in that there is an information set of some player i in F that is a union of information sets of player i in F' with the following property: any two histories h and h' in different members of the union have sub histories that are in the same information set of player i and player i's action at this information set is different in h and h'. (To relate this to the examples above, let F = F2, V = Ti, and i = 1.) Addition of a Superfluous Move According to this principle Fi is equivalent to the game F3. The argument is as follows. If in the game F3 player 1 chooses I at the start of the game then the action of player 2 is irrelevant, since it has no effect on the outcome (note the outcomes in the bottom left-hand part of the game). Thus in F3 whether player 2 is informed of player 1's choice at the start of the game should make no difference to his choice.

Formally the principle of addition of a superfluous move is the following. Let F be an extensive game, let $P(h) = t$, and let $a \in A(h)$. Suppose that for any sequence h' of actions (including the empty sequence) that follows the history (h, a) and for any $b \in A(h)$ we have

> ➤ (h, a, h') $\in$ H if and only if (h, 6, h') $\in$ H, and (h, a, h') is terminal if and only if (h, 6, h') is terminal
> ➤ if both (>, a, h') and (h, b, h') are terminal then (h, a, h') ~i(h, b, h') for all $i \in TV$
> ➤ if both (h, a, h') and (h, b, h') are nonterminal then they are in the same information set.

Then F is equivalent to the game F' that differs from F only in that

i. all histories of the form (h, c, h') for $c \in A(h)$ are replaced by the single history (h, h'),

ii. if the information set U that contains the history h in F is not a singleton then h is excluded from Ii in F', (t,>i) the player who is assigned to the history (h, h') in F' is the one who is assigned to (h, a, h') in F,

  iii. (h, h') and (h, h") are in the same information set of F' if and only if (h, a, h') and (h, a, h") are in the same information set of F, and

  4. the players' preferences are modified accordingly. (Note that F is the game that has the superfluous move, which is removed to create F'. To relate the definition to Fi and F3, let F = F3, F' = Fi, t = 2, and h = £, and let a be one of the actions of player 2.)

Example:

Formulate the principles of coalescing of moves and inflation-deflation for one-player extensive games and show that every one-player extensive game with imperfect information and no chance moves (but possibly with imperfect recall) is equivalent to a decision problem with a single nonterminal history. (The result holds even for games with chance moves, which are excluded only for simplicity.) The player restricts attention to finite extensive games in which no information set contains both a history h and some sub history of h and shows that if any two such games have the same reduced strategic form then one can be obtained from the other by a sequence of the four transformations.

5.5 Mixed and Behavioral Strategies

In earlier definition, we defined the notion of a pure strategy in an extensive game. There are two ways to model the possibility that a player's actions in such a game depend upon random factors.

Definition: A mixed strategy of player t in an extensive game {N,H,P,fc,(Ii),>i)} is a probability measure over the set of player i's pure strategies. A behavioral strategy of player i is a collection of independent probability measures, where $\beta i(Ii)$ is a probability measure over $A(Ii)$.

For any history $h \in h \in I$, and action $a \in A(h)$ we denote by $\beta i(a)$ the probability $Pi(Ii)(a)$ assigned by $A(/i)$ to the action a. Thus, as in a strategic game, a mixed strategy of player t is a probability measure over player i's set of pure strategies. By contrast, a behavioral strategy specifies a probability measure over the actions available to player t at each of his information sets. The two notions reflect two different ways in which a player might randomize: he might randomly

Mixed and Behavioral Strategies select a pure strategy, or he might plan a collection of randomizations, one for each of the points at which he has to take an action. The difference between the two notions can be appreciated by examining the game in the figure 2.2. In this game player 1 has two information sets, at each of which she has two possible actions. Thus she has four pure strategies, which assign to the information sets {0} and {(L, A), (L, B)} respectively the actions L and £, L and r, R and £, and R and r. (If you are puzzled by the last two strategies, read (or reread). A mixed strategy of player 1 is a probability distribution over these four pure strategies. By contrast, a behavioral strategy of player 1 is a pair of probability distributions, one for each information set; the first is a distribution over {L, R} and the second is a distribution over {£, r}. In describing a mixed or behavioral strategy we have used the language of the naive interpretation of actions that depend on random factors, according to which a player consciously chooses a random device.

For example, we may think of the mixed and behavioral strategies of player i as two ways of describing the other players' beliefs about player i's behavior. The other players can organize their beliefs in two ways: they can form conjectures about player i's pure strategy in the entire game (a mixed strategy), or they can form a collection of independent beliefs about player i's actions for each history after which he has to act (a behavioral strategy).

For any profile a = (<r»)i6jv of either mixed or behavioral strategies in an extensive game, we define the outcome O{a) of a to be the probability distribution over the terminal histories that results when each player i follows the precepts of Oj. For a finite game this outcome is defined precisely as follows. For any history h = (a1,...,ak) define a pure strategy Si of player i to be consistent with h if for every subhistory (a1,..., ae) of h for which P(a1,...,o')=twe have s^a1,...,ae) = ae+1. For any history h let ir^h) be the sum of the probabilities according to oy of all the pure strategies of player i that are consistent with h. (Thus for example if h is a history in which player i never moves then 7Tj(/») = 1.) Then for any profile a of mixed strategies the probability that O{a) assigns to any terminal history h is UieNu{c}Ti(h). For any profile /? of behavioral strategies the probability that O(C) assigns to the terminal history h = (a1,...,a*) is nj^1fc,(o,f...fOfc)(a\...,afc)(afc+1) (where for k = 0 the history (a1,..., ak) is the initial history).

Two (mixed or behavioral) strategies of any player are outcome – equivalent if for every collection of pure strategies of the other players the two strategies induce the same outcome. In the remainder of this section we examine the conditions under which for any mixed strategy there is an outcome-equivalent behavioral strategy and vice versa; we show, in particular, that this is so in any game with perfect recall. We first argue that, in a set of games that includes all those with perfect recall, for any behavioral strategy there is an outcome-equivalent mixed strategy. Consider an extensive game in which no information set contains both some history h and a history of the form (h, h') for some h' ^ 0. (Note that this condition is satisfied by any game with perfect recall; it is often included as part of the definition of an extensive game.) For every behavioral strategy /?i of any player i in such a game, the mixed strategy defined as follows is outcome-equivalent: the probability assigned to any pure strategy s< (which specifies an action Si(Ii) for every information set Ii e li) is n/<eij/3i(/i)(si(/i)). (Note that the derivation of this mixed strategy relies on the assumption that the collection (Pi(Ii)) ueii is independent. Note also that in a game in which some information set contains histories of the form h and (h, h') with h' ^ 0 there may be a behavioral strategy for which there is no equivalent mixed strategy: in the game.

Here the behavioral strategy that assigns probability p € U to a generates the outcomes (a, a), (a, b), and b with probabilities p2, pl, and p0 respectively, a distribution that cannot be duplicated by any mixed strategy.)

We claim that & is outcome-equivalent to at. Let s^i be a collection of pure strategies for the players other than i. Let h be a terminal history. If h includes moves that are inconsistent with s~i then the probability of h is zero under both &i and /?j. Now assume that all the moves of players other than t in h are consistent with s_j. If h includes a move after a subhistory h' € /j of h that is inconsistent with Oj then /3<(/j) assigns probability zero to this move, and thus the probability of h according to Pi is zero. Finally, if h is consistent with Oi then iTi(h') > 0 for all subhistories h' of h and the probability of h according to Pi is the product of iTi(h', a)/iTi(h') over all (/»', a) that are sub histories of h; this product is iTi(h), the probability of h according to <7j.

In a game with imperfect recall there may be a mixed strategy for which there is no outcome-equivalent behavioral strategy, as the one-player game with imperfect recall in Figure 2.2 shows. Consider the mixed strategy in which player 1 chooses LL with probability | and RR with probability P(h). The outcome of this strategy is the probability distribution (|, 0,0, |) over the terminal histories. This outcome cannot be achieved by any behavioral strategy: the behavioral strategy $((p, 1 - p), (q, 1 - q))$ induces a distribution over the terminal histories in which LR has zero probability only if either p = 0 or q = 1, in which case the probability of either LL or RR is zero.

5.6 Nash Equilibrium

A Nash equilibrium in mixed strategies of an extensive game is (as before) a profile a* of mixed strategies with the property that for every player t € N we have O{a*_i,Gi) £i 0{o*_i,Oi) for every mixed strategy at of player i. For finite games an equivalent definition of a mixed strategy equilibrium is that every pure strategy in the support of each player's mixed strategy is a best response to the strategies of the other players. A Nash equilibrium in behavioral strategies is defined analogously. By the proposition, the two definitions are equivalent for games with perfect recall. For games with imperfect recall they are not equivalent, as the game the player is indifferent among all her mixed strategies, which yield her a payoff of 0, while the behavioral strategy that assigns probability p to a yields her a payoff. Her the arugment is that the notion of Nash equilibrium is often unsatisfactory in extensive games with perfect information and we introduce the notion of subgame perfect equilibrium to deal with the problems.

5.7 Applications using Quality of Service approach

The emergence of multimedia applications in communications has generated the need to provide mobile quality-of-service (QoS) support in ad hoc networks, and such applications require a stable path to guarantee QoS requirements. However, the topology of ad hoc networks is highly dynamic due to the unpredictable node mobility. In addition, wireless channel bandwidth is limited. So, QoS provisioning in such networks is complex and challenging.

QoS routing usually involves two tasks: collecting and maintaining up-to-date state information about the network and finding feasible paths for a connection based on its QoS requirements. Many approaches currently exist to perform QoS routing, most of which consist of routing across the Network layer of the OSI model only. Some approaches utilize both the Network and Data link layer but do not consider the cross layer behaviors. This makes quantifying the QoS parameters difficult and leads to considerations of QoS but does not guarantee QoS. To address this problem, appropriate cross-layer cooperation is required. Adaptive QoS schemes provide

QoS information by factoring the impacts of node mobility and lower-layer link parameters into QoS performance.

Most QoS approaches tend to focus on only one QoS parameter (e.g., packet loss, end-to-end delay, and bandwidth). For example, while many of the QoS-related schemes are successful in reducing packet loss by adding redundancy in the packet, they do this at the expense of end-to-end delay. Because packet loss and end-to-end delay are inversely related, it may not be possible to find a path that simultaneously satisfies the delay, packet loss, and bandwidth constraints. Some proposed QoS routing algorithms do consider multiple metrics, but without considering cross-layer cooperation. Multipath routing is another type of QoS routing that has received much attention, since it can provide load balancing, fault tolerance, and higher aggregate bandwidth. Although this approach decreases packet loss and end-to-end delay, it is only efficient and reliable if a relationship can be found between the number of paths and QoS constraints.

Adaptive QoS is a cross-layer cooperation mechanism that supports adaptive multipath routing with multiple QoS constraints in an ad hoc network. The cross-layermechanism provides information on link performance for the QoS routing. It treats traffic distribution, wireless link characteristics, and node mobility in an integrated fashion. That is, it reflects the impacts of lower-layer parameters on QoS performance in higher layers, with emphasis on translating these parameters into QoS parameters for the higher-layer connections. Amultiobjective optimization algorithm is used to calculate routing parameters using the cross-layer mechanism. These parameters are adapted to the current network status, determining the number of routing paths and code parity lengths for Forward Error Correction (FEC). In addition, a traffic engineering strategy is used to evenly distribute traffic over multiple paths.

To implement an adaptive multipath routing scheme, three functions distributed in different parts of the network are needed. First, a modified dynamic source routing function is needed. It handles route discovery and collecting the local QoS-related information along the selected routes. Second, there is a local statistical computation and link monitoring function located in each node. This function is used to support the above routing function. It will manage and build the local routing information in each node, which includes a QoS-related table. The third function will be in charge of the final decision-making process. The adaptive routing parameters are derived from the decision-making algorithm based on the QoS constraints. They are the number N of selected paths, parity length k of the FEC, code and the set {R} of the traffic distribution rates on each path. With these functions, adaptive multipath QoS routing is implemented.

QoS requirements can be based on either a delay or a delay and bandwidth requirement, or a packet loss requirement. FEC parity length is derived from the difference between the QoS delay requirement and the average delay on selected paths under the packet-loss constraint. Average packet loss under this FEC scheme is achieved by using multiple routing paths. At the same time, the packet distribution rate on each path is determined under fair packet-loss and load-balance principles. Routing maintenance under the same QoS guarantees is achieved without increasing its computational complexity.

Routing protocols for mobile ad hoc networks

- Attacks on ad hoc network routing protocols
- Securing ad hoc network routing protocols
- Provable security for ad hoc network routing
- Secure routing in sensor networks

Attacks on ad-hoc network routing protocols:

- topology-based protocols
  - ➢ proactive
    - » distance vector based (e.g., DSDV)
    - » link-state (e.g., OLSR)
  - ➢ reactive (on-demand)
    - » distance vector based (e.g., AODV)
    - » source routing (e.g., DSR)

- position-based protocols
    - » greedy forwarding (e.g., GPSR, GOAFR)
    - » restricted directional flooding (e.g., DREAM, LAR)
  - ➢ hybrid approaches

Example of Dynamic Source Routing :

On-demand source routing protocol has two components :

  - ➢ **Route discovery:** It is based on flooding of Route Requests (RREQ) and returning Route Replies (RREP). Also it is used only when source S attempts to send a packet to destination D and
  - ➢ **Route maintenance:** It makes S able to detect route errors (e.g., if a link along that route no longer works)

5.8 Through Optimality Backpressure

Introduction

In a multi-node, multi-hop wireless, network with "unreliable" channels. Each transmission link, has an associated error probability that may vary with time due to external factors such as environment changes or user mobility. Many previous studies assume that accurate channel information is available so that error probabilities are relatively small and can be neglected. Let us consider case where precise channel information is difficult or impossible to obtain, but where simple estimates of channel quality can be made based on limited channel feedback.

Example:

Let us consider an underwater sensor network that uses acoustic channels with large propagation delays. This is a particularly challenging environment due to time varying wave ripple, complex signal reflections between surface and ground, and large delay spreads. While it may not be practical to assume that an accurate channel quality can be determined at the time of packet transmission, it is reasonable to estimate the error probability based on past signal strength values.

The problem of unreliable channels is also important in other contexts, such as mobile networks where knowledge of which receivers are within transmission range may be uncertain, or in dense ad-hoc networks where unpredictable transmissions of other nodes can act as random inter-channel interference. It is imperative to develop flexible mathematical models of such networks, and to develop robust networking strategies that exploit all system resources to operate efficiently in these extreme environments. Some of the robust algorithms are used to exploit the broadcast advantage of wireless networks. The network model includes the fact that a single packet transmission might be overheard by a subset of receiver nodes within range of the transmitter. This creates a multi-receiver diversity gain, where the probability of successful reception by at least one node within a subset of receivers can be much larger than the corresponding success probability of just one receiver alone. Hence, it is desirable to design flexible routing algorithms that do not require a single "next hop" receiver to be specified in advance. Such algorithms can dynamically adjust routing and scheduling decisions in response to the random outcome of each transmission.

Let us see the concept of backpressure routing and Lyapunov drift. It is possible to restrict attention to algorithms that do not allow redundant forwarding, without loss of optimality. The optimal packet commodity to transmit at each network node can be determined by a backpressure index that compares the current queue backlog of each commodity to the backlog in the potential receivers can be obtained. Once a packet from this optimal commodity is transmitted, the responsibility of forwarding the packet to its destination is shifted to the receiver node that maximizes the differential backlog. Responsibility is retained by the original transmitter if no suitable receivers are found on a given transmission attempt. Backpressure techniques of this type were first applied to multi-hop wireless networks, where throughput optimal algorithms were developed using Lyapunov drift theory. Lyapunov theory has since been a powerful mathematical tool for the development of stable scheduling strategies for wireless networks and switching systems, including our own work in that applies backpressure concepts to solve joint stability and performance optimization problems, including energy efficiency and fairness. Related work on energy efficient wireless scheduling is developed. The work in does not consider the broadcast advantage of wireless networks, and assumes that all transmissions are fully reliable. Work in considers backpressure in combination with network coding, and work in considers backpressure strategies for cooperative transmission (where multiple nodes transmit redundant information simultaneously for a power enhancement at the receiver). Heuristic algorithms that combine multireceiver diversity with network coding are developed in and complexity issues of cooperative transmission for line networks. We need not consider network coding or cooperative transmission and restrict attention to the multi-user diversity problem for networks with errors, as described above. It is likely that our formulation can be extended to consider more sophisticated control actions by augmenting the set of decision options available to the network controller, in which case redundant packet forwarding may be required for optimality.

Let us consider a time slotted system with slots normalized to integral units $t \in \{0,1,2,...\}$ There are N network nodes and links are labeled according to node pairs (a,b) for $(a,b) \in \{1,2,3,...N\}$. Data arrives randomly to the network in packetized units, and we let $A_n^{(c)}(t)$ represent the number of packets that exogenously arrive to network node n during slot t that are intended for delivery to network node c. All packets destined for a particular node c are defined as commodity c packets. Arrivals are assumed to be i.i.d. over timeslots, and we let $l_n^{(c)} = E\{A_n^{(c)}(t)\}$ represent the arrival rate of commodity c data into source node n (in units of packets/slot). Internal queues at each node store packets according to their commodities. Each packet is assumed to have an appropriate header field with commodity and packet number identifiers. At the most one packet can be transmitted from any given node during a single timeslot, and let $m_n(t)$ represent the number of packets transmitted by node n during slot t (where $m_n(t)e(0,1)$). Each packet transmission is assumed to expend a constant amount of power P_{tran}, and is successfully received by the other nodes of the network according to reception probabilities $q_{nk}(t)$ (for n,k $e\{1,2,3,...N\}$). These probabilities may be time-varying due to changing environmental conditions and/or network mobility. Assuming orthogonality on channel, so that these probabilities do not depend on the transmission decisions made at other nodes. To allow for the possibility of an underlying time division (TDMA) or random access structure that enables this orthogonality and thus the transmission opportunities at each node n are determined by a 0/1 process $X_n(t)$. Specifically, $X_n(t) = 1$ if and only if node n is allowed to transmit during slot t, and is 0 else. The $X_n(t)$ process enables the following network models:

- **Unrestricted Scheduling:** $X_n(t) = 1$ for all n $e\{1,2,...N\}$ and all t, so that each node can transmit on any slot. Transmissions are assumed to be orthogonal.

- **Restricted TDMA or Random Access:** $X_n(t) = 1$ only at pre-scheduled (or random) times that ensure channel orthogonality. This is useful as it is common to a program fixed or pseudo-random schedule of transmission opportunities into each node of an ad-hoc wireless network.

We treat $X_n(t)$ as a background MAC process that is chosen in advance and given to the higher network layers as a fixed or pseudo-random time schedule. Hence, design of $X_n(t)$ is not part of our control plane, and the $X_n(t)$ processes are not influenced by our routing and scheduling decisions. Optimality is thus measured with respect to the given $X_n(t)$ processes, and different processes may lead to different overall network performance. By the definition of the network topology state process $S(t)$ as the collective process of all node transmission capabilities and link conditions at time t, so that transmission opportunities and link probabilities can be determined as functionals of $S(t)$. That is, we have:

$$X_n(t) = {}^\wedge X_n(t)\,(S(t))$$
$$q_{nk}(t) = {}^\wedge q_{nk}(S(t)).$$

Let $K_n(t)$ represent the set consisting of all potential receivers for node n during slot t (which can potentially change from slot to slot if the network is mobile). The set $K_n(t)$ can generally contain all N-1 other network nodes.

Although it typically has a much smaller size and consists only of those nodes within realistic transmission range of node n. Error events for a single packet transmission can be correlated over various links, and hence a more complete characterization of each transmitter n is given by probabilities $q_n W_n(t)$, where n is a subset of nodes within the receiver set $K_n(t)$, and $q_n W_n(t)$ represents the probability that the set of all nodes that successfully receive the packet transmitted by node n is exactly given by the subset n. This probability is also determined as a functional of the topology state process. That is,

$$q_n W_n(t) = {}^\wedge q_n W_n(S(t))$$

The above probabilities only concern error events on links from the same outgoing node n. The error events of different packet transmissions from different nodes may also be correlated, and such additional correlations in principle are also determined by the topology state process $S(t)$. However, we shall find that error correlations between different nodes are irrelevant to network capacity and optimal control. For analytical purposes, the network topology state $S(t)$ is assumed to take values in a finite (but arbitrarily large) state space S. For each state seS, packet successes are independent with probabilities $^\wedge q_n W_n(s)$ over all slots t in which $S(t) = s$.

This formula supports all traffic (whenever possible), while maintaining average power cost as small as possible. Specifically, the requirement of the network be rate stable, so that the long term average rate of delivering packets to their destinations is equal to the input rate of exogenous sources.

5.9 General Utility Optimization

A computer optimization utility will optimize the computer so it performs at its peak performance. Some of the utilities are very useful for computer performance. The utilities below have been reviewed and are recommended to increase the computer speed and fix computer and registry errors. The optimization utility can perform a variety of tasks to keep the computer running smoothly and at its top performance on all levels of possible enhancements that can be made to speed up the system. Here is a list of some of the possible fixes and enhancements that can be made to the computer to increase the performance.

- ➢ Optimize Computer Registry
- ➢ Increase Internet Speed
- ➢ Hard Drive Defrag
- ➢ Increase Computer Speed
- ➢ Increase Boot Time
- ➢ Optimize System Settings
- ➢ Fix Computer Errors
- ➢ Update System Drivers

Utilities:

Some of the Utilities that are available in the market are as follows:

> PC Matic is a computer optimization program that does a bit more than just optimize your PC for speed. The utility also protects the computer from known security threats that may slow down and harm the system. PC Matic does a high Threat security test, has malware detection, removes junk files and caplets, updates drivers, eliminates registry errors and even gives you a detailed system specification report.

Energy consumption is a main issue of concern in wireless networks. Energy minimization increases the time that networks' nodes work properly without recharging or substituting batteries. Another criterion for network performance is data transmission rate which is usually quantified by a network utility function. There exists an inherent tradeoff between these criteria and enhancing one of them can deteriorate the other one. In this paper, we consider both Network Utility Maximization (NUM) and energy minimization in a bi-criterion optimization problem. The problem is formulated for Random Access (RA) Medium Access Control (MAC) for ad-hoc networks. First, we optimize performance of the MAC and define utility as a monotonically increasing function of link throughputs. We investigate the optimal tradeoff between energy and utility in this part. In the second part, we define utility as a function of end to end rates and optimize MAC and transport layers simultaneously. We calculate optimal persistence probabilities and end-to-end rates. Finally, by means of duality theorem, we decompose the problem into smaller sub problems, which are solved at node and network layers separately. This decomposition avoids need for a central unit while sustaining benefits of layering.

5.10 Capacity Region

Suppose arrivals $A_i(t)$ are independent and identically distributed (i.i.d.) over timeslots, and let $\lambda_i = E\{A_i(t)\}$ represent the packet arrival rate of stream i (for each $i \in \{1,2,\ldots,N\}$. Let $\lambda = \lambda_1, \lambda_2, \ldots \lambda_N$) represent the arrival rate vector. The network capacity region Λ is the closure of the set of all rate vectors λ for which a stabilizing algorithm exists. For a system of 2 queues (N = 2), the capacity region is given by all rate vectors (λ_1, λ_2) that satisfy:

$$\lambda 1 \leq q1; \lambda 2 \leq q2$$
$$\lambda 1 + \lambda 2 \leq q1 + (1 - q1)q2$$

These inequalities are clearly necessary for stability, as otherwise one or both queues would have an input rate that exceeds the transmission rate capabilities of the system. It is not difficult to show that any rate vector $(\lambda_1; \lambda_2)$ interior to this region can be stabilized. The capacity region for a system of N queues is the set of all rate vectors $\lambda = (\lambda_1, \lambda_2, \ldots, \lambda_N)$ that satisfy the inequalities:

$$\sum_{i \in I} \lambda i \leq 1 - \prod i \in I (1 - qi)$$

for each non-empty subset of indices $I \subset \{1, 2, \ldots, N\}$. Thus, the capacity region is described by a set of $(2^N - 1)$ inequality constraints. An alternate characterization of the capacity region can be given in terms of all possible expected transmission rate vectors that can be achieved by a stationary randomized scheduling policy, as shown below.

Lemma 1: (Stationary Randomized Policies) A rate vector $\lambda = (\lambda 1, \lambda 2, \ldots, \lambda N)$ is in the capacity region Λ if and only if there exists a stationary control strategy that chooses a transmission rate vector $\mu(t) = (\mu 1(t), \mu 2(t), \ldots, \mu N(t))$ as a (potentially random) function of the observed channel state vector $S(t) = (S1(t), \ldots, SN(t))$ such that $\mu(t)$ satisfies

$$\sum_{i=1}^{n} \mu i(t) \leq 1$$

for all t, and such that the expected transmission rate yields: $E\{\mu i(t)\} = \lambda i$ for all $i \in \{1, \ldots, N\}$ The expectation above is with respect to the stationary distribution for the channel state vector S(t) and the potentially random transmission decision that depends on S(t).

Note that in the special case of a symmetric system where qi = q for all i∈{1,2,...,N}, then the largest symmetric rate vector $(\lambda,\lambda,...,\lambda)$ that is in the capacity region is given by the vector with $\lambda i = r_N/N$ for all i∈{1,2,...,N}, where r_N is the probability that at least one link is in the ON state during a timeslot

$$r_N \triangleq 1-(1-q)^N$$

Thus, the optimization helps in improvising the quality of service in computer network for the service deployment of various scenarios. It can be used to optimize the functionality of network service through utilities and also to measure the capacity.

www.ingramcontent.com/pod-product-compliance
Lightning Source LLC
Chambersburg PA
CBHW040953110726
48007CB00001B/8